VALENTINES DAY
Coloring Book

DISCOVER AND ENJOY A VARIETY OF COLORING PAGES FOR KIDS

This is a Bleed Through Page If You Are Using a Coloring Marker or Pen!

Bold Illustrations
COLORING BOOKS

This is a Bleed Through Page If You Are Using a Coloring Marker or Pen!

Bold Illustrations
COLORING BOOKS

This is a Bleed Through Page If You Are Using a Coloring Marker or Pen!

Bold Illustrations

COLORING BOOKS

Happy Valentine's Day

This is a Bleed Through Page If You Are Using a Coloring Marker or Pen!

Bold Illustrations
COLORING BOOKS

This is a Bleed Through Page If You Are Using a Coloring Marker or Pen!

Bold Illustrations
COLORING BOOKS

Together Forever !

This is a Bleed Through Page If You Are Using a Coloring Marker or Pen!

Bold Illustrations

COLORING BOOKS

This is a Bleed Through Page If You Are Using a Coloring Marker or Pen!

Bold Illustrations
COLORING BOOKS

This is a Bleed Through Page If You Are Using a Coloring Marker or Pen!

Bold Illustrations
COLORING BOOKS

This is a Bleed Through Page If You Are Using a Coloring Marker or Pen!

Bold Illustrations
COLORING BOOKS

14 FEBRUARY

This is a Bleed Through Page If You Are Using a Coloring Marker or Pen!

Bold Illustrations
COLORING BOOKS

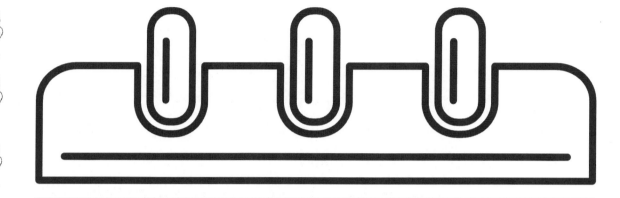

This is a Bleed Through Page If You Are Using a Coloring Marker or Pen!

Bold Illustrations
COLORING BOOKS

This is a Bleed Through Page If You Are Using a Coloring Marker or Pen!

Bold Illustrations
COLORING BOOKS

This is a Bleed Through Page If You Are Using a Coloring Marker or Pen!

Bold Illustrations
COLORING BOOKS

This is a Bleed Through Page If You Are Using a Coloring Marker or Pen!

Bold Illustrations
COLORING BOOKS

This is a Bleed Through Page If You Are Using a Coloring Marker or Pen!

Bold Illustrations
COLORING BOOKS

This is a Bleed Through Page If You Are Using a Coloring Marker or Pen!

Bold Illustrations
COLORING BOOKS

This is a Bleed Through Page If You Are Using a Coloring Marker or Pen!

Bold Illustrations
COLORING BOOKS

This is a Bleed Through Page If You Are Using a Coloring Marker or Pen!

Bold Illustrations
COLORING BOOKS

This is a Bleed Through Page If You Are Using a Coloring Marker or Pen!

Bold Illustrations
COLORING BOOKS

Love you

This is a Bleed Through Page If You Are Using a Coloring Marker or Pen!

Bold Illustrations
COLORING BOOKS

This is a Bleed Through Page If You Are Using a Coloring Marker or Pen!

Bold Illustrations
COLORING BOOKS

This is a Bleed Through Page If You Are Using a Coloring Marker or Pen!

Bold Illustrations
COLORING BOOKS

This is a Bleed Through Page If You Are Using a Coloring Marker or Pen!

Bold Illustrations
COLORING BOOKS

This is a Bleed Through Page If You Are Using a Coloring Marker or Pen!

Bold Illustrations
COLORING BOOKS

This is a Bleed Through Page If You Are Using a Coloring Marker or Pen!

Bold Illustrations
COLORING BOOKS

This is a Bleed Through Page If You Are Using a Coloring Marker or Pen!

Bold Illustrations
COLORING BOOKS

This is a Bleed Through Page If You Are Using a Coloring Marker or Pen!

Bold Illustrations
COLORING BOOKS

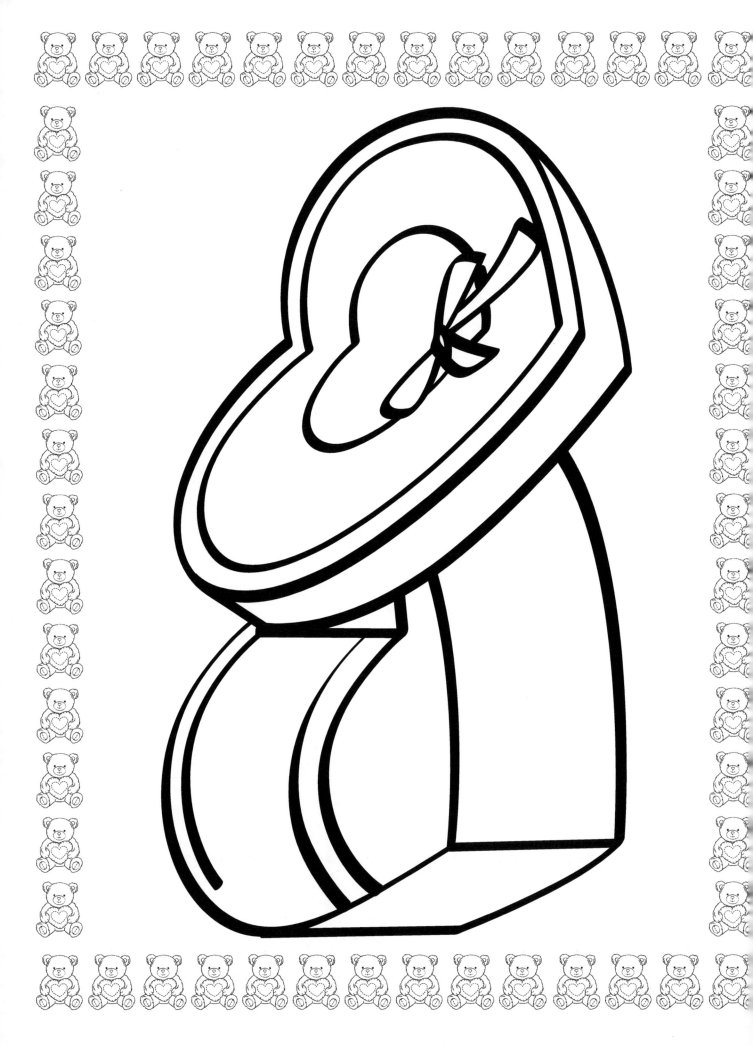

This is a Bleed Through Page If You Are Using a Coloring Marker or Pen!

Bold Illustrations
COLORING BOOKS

This is a Bleed Through Page If You Are Using a Coloring Marker or Pen!

Bold Illustrations
COLORING BOOKS

This is a Bleed Through Page If You Are Using a Coloring Marker or Pen!

Bold Illustrations
COLORING BOOKS

This is a Bleed Through Page If You Are Using a Coloring Marker or Pen!

Bold Illustrations
COLORING BOOKS

This is a Bleed Through Page If You Are Using a Coloring Marker or Pen!

Bold Illustrations
COLORING BOOKS

This is a Bleed Through Page If You Are Using a Coloring Marker or Pen!

Bold Illustrations

COLORING BOOKS

This is a Bleed Through Page If You Are Using a Coloring Marker or Pen!

Bold Illustrations
COLORING BOOKS

This is a Bleed Through Page If You Are Using a Coloring Marker or Pen!

Bold Illustrations
COLORING BOOKS

This is a Bleed Through Page If You Are Using a Coloring Marker or Pen!

Bold Illustrations
COLORING BOOKS

This is a Bleed Through Page If You Are Using a Coloring Marker or Pen!

Bold Illustrations
COLORING BOOKS

This is a Bleed Through Page If You Are Using a Coloring Marker or Pen!

Bold Illustrations
COLORING BOOKS

This is a Bleed Through Page If You Are Using a Coloring Marker or Pen!

Bold Illustrations
COLORING BOOKS

This is a Bleed Through Page If You Are Using a Coloring Marker or Pen!

Bold Illustrations
COLORING BOOKS

Made in the USA
Las Vegas, NV
22 January 2022

42120258R00046